Ben Franklin
and the
MAGIC SQUARES

A Math Reader

by Frank Murphy
illustrated by Richard Walz

Random House 🏠 New York

Learning to Read, Step by Step!

Ready to Read   Preschool–Kindergarten
• big type and easy words • rhyme and rhythm • picture clues
For children who know the alphabet and are eager to begin reading.

Reading with Help   Preschool–Grade 1
• basic vocabulary • short sentences • simple stories
For children who recognize familiar words and sound out new words with help.

Reading on Your Own   Grades 1–3
• engaging characters • easy-to-follow plots • popular topics
For children who are ready to read on their own.

Reading Paragraphs   Grades 2–3
• challenging vocabulary • short paragraphs • exciting stories
For newly independent readers who read simple sentences with confidence.

Ready for Chapters   Grades 2–4
• chapters • longer paragraphs • full-color art
For children who want to take the plunge into chapter books but still like colorful pictures.

STEP INTO READING® is designed to give every child a successful reading experience. The grade levels are only guides. Children can progress through the steps at their own speed, developing confidence in their reading, no matter what their grade.

Remember, a lifetime love of reading starts with a single step!

AMIGOS SCHOOL LIBRARY
Cambridge, MA 02139

*For the most magically magical magic souls I know,
Griffin and Chase!—F.M.*

*For my three terrific cousins,
Tyler, Colby, and Carter Scruggs—R.W.*

Author Acknowledgments: *Thanks to Mallory Loehr, Heidi Kilgras, and Shana Corey for
believing in me, and especially Mallory for her support, guidance, and collaboration.
With many thanks to Roy Goodman, curator of the American Philosophical Society in
Philadelphia, for his expertise on the life of Ben Franklin.*

www.stepintoreading.com

Educators and librarians, for a variety of teaching tools, visit us at
www.randomhouse.com/teachers

Library of Congress Cataloging-in-Publication Data
Murphy, Frank, 1952–
Ben Franklin and the magic squares / by Frank Murphy ; illustrated by Richard Walz.
    p.   cm. — (Step into reading: a math reader. A step 4 book)
SUMMARY: Shows how Benjamin Franklin, inventor, writer, and scientist, created a puzzle called
the magic square to keep from being bored while serving as a clerk for the Pennsylvania
Assembly. Includes step-by-step instructions for creating your own magic squares.
ISBN 0-375-80621-0 (trade) — ISBN 0-375-90621-5 (lib. bdg.)
1. Franklin, Benjamin, 1706–1790—Juvenile fiction. [1. Franklin, Benjamin, 1706–1790—Fiction.
2. Number games—Fiction. 3. Mathematical recreations—Fiction.]
I. Walz, Richard, ill. II. Title. III. Series: Step into reading: a math reader. Step 4 book.
PZ7.M95335 Be 2003 [Fic]—dc21 2002013651

Printed in the United States of America   16 15 14 13 12 11 10 9 8 7

STEP INTO READING, RANDOM HOUSE, and the Random House colophon are registered trademarks of
Random House, Inc.

Over 200 years ago, when America was just 13 colonies, there lived a super smart guy. You may have heard of him. His name was Benjamin Franklin. But most people called him Ben.

This story is about how Ben invented magic squares. But first, there are a few things you need to know about this great man . . .

Ben Franklin wasn't smart for nothing. He put his big brain to good use. He was always thinking and writing and inventing cool things—even when he was a kid.

When he was 11 years old, Ben jumped into a lake holding on to a kite.

The kite was pulled by the wind.

Ben was pulled by the kite.

The kite flew a whole mile with Ben holding on tight!

That same year, Ben wanted to swim faster than anyone. So he made flippers for his hands and feet.

They worked!

Flippers, 1717

People still use a version of Ben's flippers today.

As Ben grew older, he kept thinking and writing and inventing. When he was 23, he wrote and printed a newspaper called *The Pennsylvania Gazette*.
People loved it!

The Pennsylvania Gazette, first edition, 1729

Poor Richard's Almanac, first edition, 1732

When he was 26, Ben wrote and printed
a book called _Poor Richard's Almanac_.

An _almanac_ is a book of useful
information, from weather predictions and
advertisements to important dates. Ben's
almanacs had even more things in them.
There were witty sayings (_witty_ means
"clever") and fun puzzles (you know what
fun means).

When Ben was 36, he invented a special stove. It kept homes warmer than a fire in a fireplace and burned less wood. Everyone was amazed!

Franklin stove, 1742

People still use Franklin stoves today!

Ben never outgrew his love of kites. When he was 46, he tied a key to a kite string and . . .

. . . flew the kite in a thunderstorm!

This was *not* a safe thing to do. But Ben *did* find out that lightning was made of electricity.

Experiments with electricity, 1752

And electricity is used today as well!

Once Ben even invented a special
rocking chair. It had a fan on top. Ben
rocked back and forth and the fan swished
this way and that. It really kept the flies
off his head!

No one else ever used *this* invention—
not in Ben's time and not in ours!

Over the years, Ben also started
America's first library,

The Library Company
of Philadelphia, 1731

America's first fire station,

Union Fire Company, 1736

and America's first hospital, too!

Pennsylvania Hospital, 1751

He even helped Thomas Jefferson write and *re*write the Declaration of Independence in 1776.

To DO

1. Meet with T.J.
2. Fix kite
3. ~~Invent~~ telephone
   maybe later!
4. Print almanac
5. Make up 5 jokes
6. Play game
   with William
7. Buy present for
   Deborah

So you get the idea that Ben Franklin was a super busy guy. Right?

Then you are ready for the story of the magic squares.

It all started in the middle of Ben's life in 1736. That year he became a clerk for the Pennsylvania Colonial Assembly. The *Assembly* was a group of men who made laws for the colony of Pennsylvania. A *clerk* was the person who kept track of all the important decisions they made.

The guys in the Assembly chose Ben
to be a clerk because they knew he was
super smart and a great writer!

Ben listened carefully to the men in the Assembly. He couldn't write anything down until they agreed on something. So Ben waited and waited.

For days, he listened to long arguments about which laws were good and which laws were bad.

For more days, Ben listened to fights about taxes and bills.

And for even *more* days, Ben listened to disagreements about numbers and money, city streets and state laws.

Until one day . . .

The members of the Assembly were not happy.

"Mr. Franklin!" one of them said loudly.

Ben woke up. He was very
embarrassed.
"I am so sorry!" he said.

Everyone went back to work.

The men argued.

Ben listened and listened. He kept his ears open and his eyes open. It was very hard.

Day turned into night, and the assemblymen still argued.

Ben found out it was easier to stay awake if his hands were busy. He twiddled his thumbs.

He tickled his nose with his quill pen.

He dipped his pen in ink and started to doodle.

Ben doodled people.

Ben doodled new inventions.

Ben even doodled a doodle of his pet squirrel, Skugg.

The men in the assembly were still arguing. So Ben decided to doodle a math puzzle.

He drew a square. Then he drew two lines going up and down and two lines going left and right. This made nine boxes in one big box.

Ben wrote a different number in each box.

5	7	3
2	4	9
8	1	6

He stared at the box of numbers. He waited for an idea to pop into his head.

Ben noticed something! When he added the numbers in the first row, they equaled 15. When he added the numbers in the first column, they equaled 15 as well.

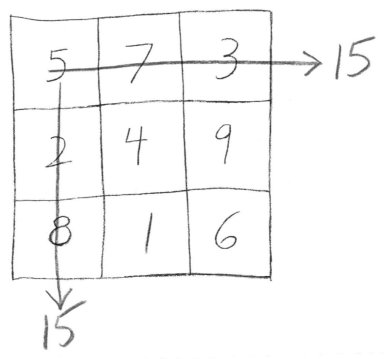

Now Ben wondered if he could make the numbers add up to 15 no matter which row or column he picked. What if they even added up to 15 in a diagonal line? That would be more than a math puzzle, it would be a magic square!

Ben started arranging the numbers . . .

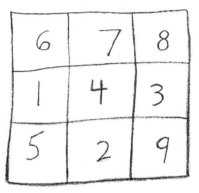

. . . sorting the numbers . . .

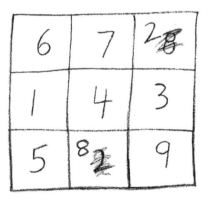

. . . and *re*arranging the numbers!

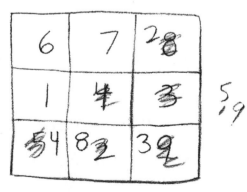

Ben was thinking so hard about his
magic square that he was not sleepy at all!

Finally, he saw what needed to be done!

First he wrote a 1 in the center box of the top row.

Next he wrote a 2 in the last box of the third row.

He wrote a 3 in the first box of the second row.

Then Ben wrote a 4 in the bottom box of the first column. He wrote a 5 in the box in the center. Then a 6 in the third box of the first row.

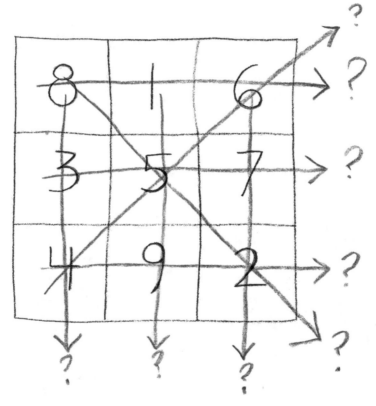

Under the 6, Ben wrote a 7.

Ben wrote an 8 inside the first box of the top row. Finally, he wrote a 9 in the only box left.

Was it a magic square?

Ben started adding.

Each row and column added up to 15.

Even the diagonals added up to 15!

"It's magically magic!" Ben shouted.
He had made a magic square!

After that, Ben never dozed off at the Assembly again.

Instead, he doodled magic squares until either the assemblymen finally made a decision *or* . . .

How about lights on all the streets so people can see at night?

Streetlight bill enacted, 1751. Renewed 1756.

. . . he had a good idea of his own for them!

Ben went on to publish his magic
squares in his newspapers and almanacs.
People loved figuring out the magic
answers.

And they still do!

MAKE YOUR OWN MAGIC SQUARE

A. Draw a square. Draw a tic-tac-toe board inside the square.

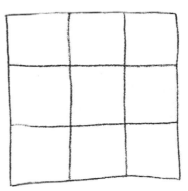

B. Start with the number 1. Put it in the middle of the top row.

C. Put the number 2 in the box that is directly above and to the right of the 1.

Okay. Wait—hold it! You're probably saying, "There is no box above and to the right of the 1." That's true. So here's what you do: Since there is no box above the 1, drop down to the bottom of the column that holds the 1. *Now* move one square to the right and there you go! Put your number 2 there!

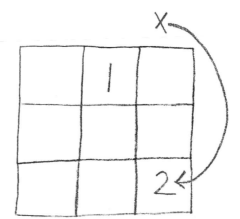

D. Okay, now you're ready for the number 3. So repeat step C: Look for the box above and to the right. Move up one row and then . . . yep, you are correct! There is no box to the right!

What do you do? Move that 3 to the beginning of the row above the 2! Like this!

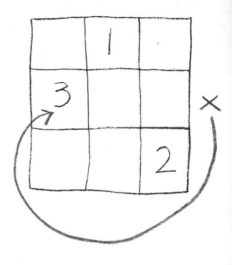

E. Now you are ready for the number 4. Just look above and to the right again!

Yes, you're correct again! There is already a number in the box. So what do you do? Anytime there is a number already in the box you want, just put the next number in the box below the number you just wrote. So put the 4 below the 3.

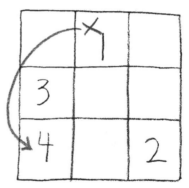

F. Now for the numbers 5 to 9! Always look for the box above and to the right.

If you get stuck, go step by step. If there is no box above, drop down to the bottom of the column, *then* move to the right. If there is no box to the right, move to the beginning of the row. And so on!

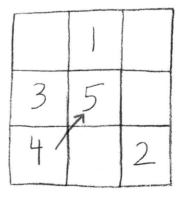

46

G. Ta-da! Your magic square! What makes it magic? Add the numbers in each of the rows. Now add each of the columns. And finally, add each of the diagonals. What do you get? 15. A perfect magic square!

There are many ways to make magic squares—big ones and little ones! Try starting with 9 and working down to 1! This time, the 9 goes in the middle of the top row, instead of the 1.

8	1	6
3	5	7
4	9	2

AUTHOR'S NOTE

Well, no one knows exactly how or exactly when Ben Franklin came up with magic squares. But we do know these things:

• He really did get bored when he was a clerk in the Pennsylvania Colonial Assembly (1736–1751).

• He definitely made magic squares in 1736 and 1737.

• He called the magic square his "most magically magical magic squares."

• He really invented and made up all the things in this book, plus a lot more!

• He really did have a pet squirrel named Skugg.